W9-BCI-643

DATE DUE

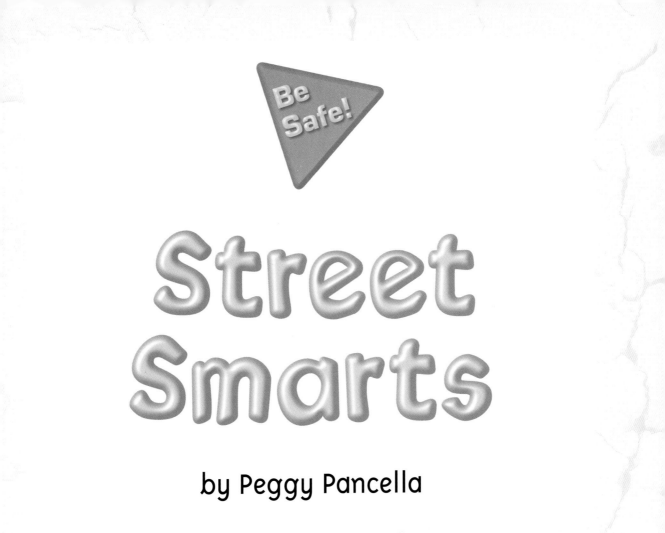

Be Safe!

Street Smarts

by Peggy Pancella

Heinemann Library
Chicago, Illinois

Designed by Heinemann Library
Page layout by Roslyn Broder
Printed and bound in China by South China Printing Co. Ltd.

09 08 07 06 05
10 9 8 7 6 5 4 3 2 1

Library of Congress Cataloging-in-Publication Data
Pancella, Peggy.
  Street smarts / Peggy Pancella.
      v. cm. -- (Be safe)
  Includes bibliographical references and index.
  Contents: What is safety? -- Get ready to ride -- Riding safely -- Plan a route -- Walking safely -- Crossing the street -- Street safety -- Dangerous places -- Strangers -- Lost! -- Finding help -- Calling for help -- Be smart and safe -- Safety tips.
  ISBN 1-4034-4933-3 (hardcover) -- ISBN 1-4034-4942-2 (pbk.)
  1. Children's accidents--Prevention--Juvenile literature. [1. Safety.] I. Title. II. Series: Pancella, Peggy. Be safe!
  HV675.5.P36 2004
  613.6--dc22

2003024067

Acknowledgments
The author and publisher are grateful to the following for permission to reproduce copyright material:
Cover photograph by Richard Hutchings/Photo Edit, Inc.
p. 4 Taxi/Getty Images; pp. 5, 16, 17 Tony Freeman/Photo Edit, Inc.; p. 6 Michelle D. Bridwell/Photo Edit, Inc.; pp. 7, 10, 12, 22, 23, 24, 25, 26, 28, 29 David Young-Wolff/Photo Edit, Inc.; pp. 8, 20, 27 Michael Newman/Photo Edit, Inc.; p. 9 Spencer Grant/Photo Edit, Inc.; p. 11 Dennis MacDonald/Photo Edit, Inc.; p. 13 Mary Steinbacher/Photo Edit, Inc.; pp. 14, 18 Davis Barber/Photo Edit, Inc.; p. 15 Bill Aron/Photo Edit, Inc.; p. 19 Jeff Greenberg/Photo Edit, Inc.; p. 21 Barbara Stitzer/Photo Edit, Inc.

Every effort has been made to contact copyright holders of any material reproduced in this book. Any omissions will be rectified in subsequent printings if notice is given to the publisher.

Contents

Some words are shown in bold, **like this.** You can find out what they mean by looking in the glossary.

What Is Safety?

It is important for everyone to stay safe. Being safe means keeping out of danger. It means staying away from things or people that could hurt you.

Safety is important in everything you do. One good time to be safe is when you ride or walk through your neighborhood. Learning some rules to follow can help you stay safe.

Get Ready to Ride

A good way to stay safe in a car is to buckle yourself in. Babies and young children need car seats. Older children and adults should use seat belts instead.

Car seats and belts can help keep you safe in an **accident.** Even a short trip can be dangerous, so always make sure everyone is buckled up before riding.

Riding Safely

When you ride in a car, stay in your car seat or seat belt. Keep your hands and head inside the car. Playing around could cause you to get hurt.

Do not bother the driver, either. He or she needs to pay attention to the road. When the car stops, check for people or cars before opening your door to get out.

Plan a Route

Sometimes you may want to walk places by yourself. Before going out alone, plan a **route** with your parents. They can help you choose the best path to follow.

It is a good idea to practice walking your route with your parents. They can show you where to cross streets and where to go if you have trouble.

Walking Safely

When you leave home, always tell an adult where you are going and when you will return. Walking with a friend can be fun and is safer than walking alone.

Follow your **route** so you do not get lost. Use the sidewalk when you can. If you must walk in the road, stay to the left side, facing traffic. This will help drivers see you more easily.

Crossing the Street

When you cross the street, use a **crosswalk** if there is one. You can also cross at the corner. Stop at the **curb** to look and listen for traffic.

Look to the left, then right, then left again. When the road is clear, it is safe to cross. Walk quickly, but do not run! Stay **alert** while you cross.

Street Safety

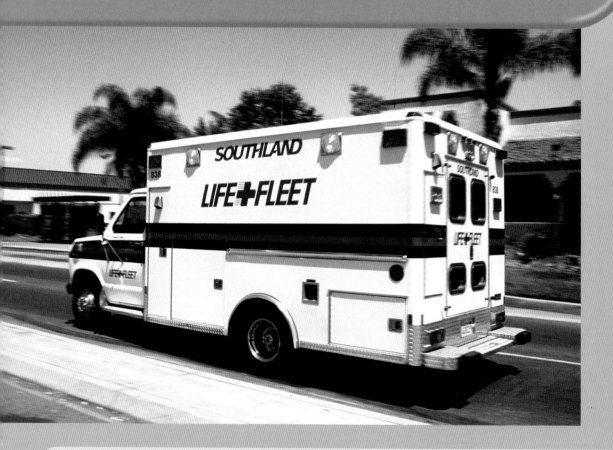

Always be careful near streets. Traffic can be dangerous. Cars and trucks are large and strong. **Emergency vehicles** travel fast. Their **sirens** and lights warn that they are coming.

Even if you do not see any cars, you should not play in the street. Never chase pets or toys into the street, either. Ask an adult for help.

Dangerous Places

Not all places are safe to walk or play. Train tracks and parking lots have **vehicles** that could hurt you. Empty buildings may be falling apart or full of trash.

Some places have "Keep Out" signs, fences, or orange cones to warn you of danger. Always stay away from places like these. Stay in well-lit areas where there are plenty of people.

DANGER
SEWAGE CONTAMINATED
BEACH AND WATER

*AVOID SHELLFISH HARVESTING, SWIMMING,
BEACH COMBING, OR OTHER CONTACT ACTIVITIES*

Strangers

Sometimes you may see people you do not know in your neighborhood. They are strangers to you. Some strangers are nice, but others could try to hurt you.

If a stranger tries to touch or talk to you, step away and tell a trusted adult. Never go anywhere with strangers. Do not take money or other gifts from them, either.

Lost!

Even the most careful people sometimes get lost. You may feel scared or upset if this happens to you. Try to stay calm and think clearly.

If someone was with you, stay where you are. The person might come back to find you. If you were alone, or if you feel unsafe, look for help right away.

Finding Help

If you feel lost or unsafe, go for help. Find a safe place with lots of people around, such as a store or **restaurant**. Look for an adult who can help.

Try to find an adult that you feel you can trust. Police officers are very helpful people. Women with children and store workers are usually safe to ask, too.

Calling for Help

Pay phones can be helpful, too. Always carry enough money for a phone call. If you know the number of a parent or trusted adult, put your money in, and dial.

If you do not have money, you can call **911** for free. Say you need help and answer the **operator's** questions. Operators can figure out where you are and send help.

Be Smart and Safe

You should be prepared whenever you walk. Wear clothing that is right for the day's weather. After dark, wear light-colored clothes and stay in well-lit areas.

Pay attention to things around you. Tell an adult if anything seems unusual or strange. Most of all, walk tall and proud. Being safe can also be fun!

Safety Tips

- Always ride safely—buckle up!

- Plan and practice a safe **route** for walking alone.

- Listen for traffic and look both ways before crossing a street. Use a **crosswalk** if you can.

- Stay away from people or places that might be dangerous. If you have a problem or something does not feel right, tell an adult you trust.

- **Memorize** important phone numbers and carry enough money to make a phone call.

Glossary

911 phone number to dial in an emergency

accident something that happens unexpectedly

alert paying attention to things around you

crosswalk place on a street where you can safely cross to the other side

curb raised edge along the side of the street

emergency sudden event that forces you to act quickly

memorize learn by heart

operator person whose job is to give help or information over the telephone

pay phone public telephone that takes money

restaurant public eating place

route path you take to get somewhere

siren kind of loud warning signal

vehicle something that carries people or supplies from one place to another

Index

RULES OF THE GAME

BASEBALL POEMS

Marjorie Maddox

Illustrated by
John Sandford

WORDSONG
Honesdale, Pennsylvania

To Anna Lee and Will, my favorite Little Leaguers
—*M.M.*

For optimistic Cubs fan Jim Wildenradt
—*J.S.*

Acknowledgments
With deep gratitude to my husband, Gary, who taught me the poetry of the game;
and to my editor, Joan Hyman, who umpired with enthusiasm and good sense
—*M.M.*

Thanks and appreciation to Clark Wildenradt, Ernie Banks, and George Jacobson
—*J.S.*

The following poems first appeared in *When the Wood Clacks Out Your Name: Baseball Poems* by Marjorie Maddox, published by Redgreene Press, 2002: "The Pitch," "Balk," "Passed Ball/Wild Pitch," "Beanball," "'Three and Two, What'll He Do?'," "Walk," "Foul Ball," "Error," "The Pop-up," "Pinch Hitter," "The Sacrifice Bunt," "Hit and Run," "The Slide," "Double Play," "Out," "Safe," "Stealing Home," and "Grand Slam."

Wordsong
An Imprint of Boyds Mills Press, Inc.
815 Church Street
Honesdale, Pennsylvania 18431
Printed in China

Library of Congress Cataloging-in-Publication Data

Maddox, Marjorie.
  Rules of the game : baseball poems / Marjorie Maddox ;
illustrations by John Sandford. — 1st ed.
    p. cm.
  ISBN 978-1-59078-603-1 (alk. paper)
  1. Baseball—Juvenile poetry. 2. Children's poetry, American.
  I. Sandford, John, ill. II. Title.
  PS3613.A284324B37 2009
  811'.6—dc22

                              2008019018

First edition

The text of this book is set in 13-point Garamond Book Condensed.
The illustrations are done in pencil.

10 9 8 7 6 5 4 3 2 1

Contents

Balk

It's a poker-face turn-on to turn,
stretch back, twist
enough to make them guess
which way to shift, push off the calves,
clip toward base. Nobody thinks
you're lying till, slip-slap on the wrist,
that arm shoots up: one more obscenity
amidst the crowd's limp moans. And then
the slow tick of men, clicking around
to the twelve- or nine- or six-o'clock
plate as you wait for the moment
to end, the possible out
ousted—or the other score
more. You cringe, cower,
back up into your crank-up,
once again let it soar.

Pitchout

It's the catcher's signal
that tells the pitcher
to hurl the ball
wide of the strike zone
and into his waiting glove.

"Gotcha!" thinks the catcher,
whose keen eyes spotted
a runner inching to steal
but now can't because
the man with a cage on his face

crushes the runner's scheme
by a quick chuck
to the second baseman,
who completes the trio's trick
and makes the tag.

The Pitch

One hundred eight stitches
  switch the swish of air
    on each celebrated sphere
      that hobnobs with the pitcher
      and catcher in closed conference.

  The circle change:
  fingers OK'ing the seams,
  ball hugged deep in the palm.
  Fingers straddle the stitches for a splitter,
    let the circle sink at the plate.
      A slider spins from the wrist like a football;
        a screwball: surprise party with a twist.
      For the rebel: the chance to scuff or spit.

    Snap here for a fastball,
      here for a curve;
        cut your fingernails square
          for a knuckler, that pigeon
          flapping awkwardly
          out the barn door of a hand.

      Never let the eyes tell
        the fingers' deception,
        the plans of the palm,
      deep-secret mathematics
    shooting great lengths
  from arm to plate.

5

The Batting Order

With 360,000 possibilities,
it's all calculations, probabilities—
here for the best all-around,
here for the cleanup hitter,
way back here for the pitcher. Or maybe
not—the mystery of batting magic
a Rubik's Cube of what nine dudes
might or might not do.
Study statistics until you're blue,
but swing true.

Choking Up on the Bat

High on the handle hurries the wood toward its whack. But Jack,
a quick crack loses the stronger smack that attacks the ball, creates a neck-
turning trek past the mound on the ground, *thwack*—like that!

The Strike Zone

The parallelogram between
armpits and knees
and the known width of home
slides up and down
with the build of the batter
and an umpire's brash verdict.
What can be lost is plenty
when the ump refuses to see
the sphere's flight as slightly above the knee
and calls it a ball instead because he saw
the pitch arrive an inch lower—
that clinches the difference
between first and back-to-the-dugout.

The Sweet Spot

knows no sting,
sings its center of percussion
six inches from the stick's end.
Resonating energy, it sounds the cosmic note.
Before you can listen, the ball is gone.

Beanball

The body, not the bat,
is the bull's-eye for the bullet holder
who bullies with intimidation,
lets loose the touted torpedo
trekking toward territory
disputed by the batter's feet.

"Three and Two, What'll He Do?"

The fine line between do and die
is an arm and its aim,
a multiple-choice motion that moves the game,
muscles of pitcher and batter
in arm-to-arm argument,
a two-man bluff or boast
that keeps the same fans guessing,
the famed boys battling,
through every sane and insane summer inning.

Passed Ball/Wild Pitch

Their seesaw with the ball
tilts in turns, alternating errors.
Whoops and *oops* are too soft
for these scuffed egos,
unbalanced by boo-boos.
Once the princes of playgrounds,
the duo now endures
their friends' childish pooh-poohs.

Batting Cage

"If at first you don't …" was meant for here.
Keep swinging till you hit sustained success.
The net will catch the ball; you do the rest.
Practice = runs = cheers.

Walk

Won by another's bad aim,
the luxury of slow motion,
a step-by-step to first,
everyone watching.

Forget speed,
the long arc of a line drive
with little time to tag the bags.

Instead
this ponderous gait to base:
the power of paradox,
earned leisure that quickens the game.

A Strike

by any other name is a (sometimes) foul, is a swing
that swats only air, is doing nothing when the ball's right there—
three times is an out is an out is an out.

Foul Ball

The wayward one,
it rebels against bat and air,
just enough off aim to gain attention.
Some in the stands reach out, grabbing, wanting;
others cover their heads, want nothing
to do with such misconduct.
There is no end to the ball's stalling,
three, four, five fouls and all "Strike two!"
while we wait for salvation
in a real hit or out, not this foul purgatory.

The View from the Dugout

can be full of glare and close calls
on the first-base side.
Try TV after this and you'll quit
that electronic imitation.
Here the game's spread out In Living Color
with bench commentators calling the play-by-play
with or without agreement from the umpire.
No channel surfing. What you see is
what continues for the inning.
To adjust your picture,
jump in.

In the Bullpen

Waiting's the game in this foul territory.
What the arm engineers here could save
or scathe what's left of the inning
or the season. *When* is the question;
"Warm up!" the command;
windup, leg lift, thrust, follow-through
the practiced reaction.

Relief Pitcher

Relief for the weary arm,
the blurry-eyed,
the back begging for rest,
you rescue the worn down.

Or, replacement for the reckless
and the downright no-longer-good,
you denounce all runs
and rack up the strikes,
win high-fives from the Fans of the Nine.

Or, hero of the injured,
you fail to make the save;
your savored chance just fades away.
Though you hurl your best pitch,
the other team's score
soars more.

Home Run

Anything less is a slice.
Hungry, you want the whole pie.
With the ball out of sight past the wall,
you crave every last crumb of the run
as you trot with arms held high
from plate to plate to plate,
all the way back to home,
your fans deliciously happy,
stuffed full of satisfaction,
unable to ask for one bite more
of such scrumptious summer joy.

Designated Hitter

A dynamo over dirt,
you wield the wood with a whoosh,
wallop that once-white sphere
with a *Yikes!* that flies it fast and furious
toward a field you won't defend,
your one-job, star status here—
hero at home plate.

17

Balance

"Down and ready" does it all:
from this crouch, you
                                    dive,
break,
                    or dodge,
    the ball reaching for your fingertips,
ready for your say-so. You can   leap
                                    or scoop
        your way across the field, fast-delivering the ball
to the cutoff man.   Now!
        Down and ready!
                        Here it comes.
        The ball.

Up High

A skyscraper, a crane, a giraffe,
        a trapeze artist stretching for her swing,
                a daredevil acrobat, a high-leaping dancer, or better yet—
                the ballplayer grabbing what she dreams.

Error

For its guilt,
the defense cannot rest
or erase its wrongdoing,
its Charlie Brown blunder
replayed for the coach-potato bunch.
It's botched, bungled, fumbled, flubbed,
and there's no undoing baseball erratum.
Best move on, keep the brain on the ball.

Grounder

Bashed midseam, the sphere rotates with top spin, hop-skips on artificial turf,
or bounces across the grass where a fielder charges, scoops it up, swooshes it again
where it belongs, back into focused flight toward the hoped-for out
that everyone's been forecasting since bat hit ball.

Collision

Two players with equal
　　　　　　and opposite forces and
　　　　Crash!
　　　　　　Bam!
　　　　　　in the race to the ball
　　　that nobody called
　　　　　　in time to avoid the crunch
　　of shoulder and limb,
　　　　　　head and back
with the teammate who blocked
　　　　　　—by accident—
the ball you were going to claim
　　　　　　before *Yeow!*
　　　　　　got in the way
　　　and ruined our run-free day.

The Pop-up

Disastrous beauty,
its peak such clean geometrical perfection,
the sudden glorious dive into the player's glove
a sleek vertical arc,
all eyes on the honored orb
humming toward capture:
pathos in the park.

Infield Fly Rule

An insurance policy for runners,
it naysays the double play on days the bases
are claimed by two or three players.
Catch the ball or drop it,
it's still one out per customer.
"Infield fly!" the ump yells
to a crowd ever confused by his rulings.

Catch on Bound

Rewind to last century when your mitt
could get a second chance.

No way these days!
If you covet an out, nab that catch now

or not at all. Baseball's not

        Bounce
First   or   Fly!

There's only time for one try.

        Come on,
            stretch high!

Pinch Hitter

A pressure cooker about to bust
out—a ball bursting past lights—
or inward—a strike
crumbling confidence.
For the dying,
a diamond-sized last-ditch effort,
heroically blasting the team into the game.
For the batter, simply the glory
or the gore.

The Line Drive

Fast, straight, head-high,
a sharp swing of invisible string on which the ball careens
to a surprised shortstop.

Or a limbo line of speed stretched taut between
the batter's clack and the fielder's background of green.

The shortest distance in this baseball universe
between right here and

                                        way out there.

Hit and Run

Think camouflage, think stealth,
wind not in the jungle trees
but in the swing of a bat not yet connected to ball.
In that sound, in that half-second
when feet decide before brain,
strategy planned and won by toes and centimeters,
the strong subterfuge of survivors
sneaking past enemy territory.

The Sacrifice Bunt

Here humility makes the hero,
     squaring off to fail his own trail to base.
          He entices the ball with his bat,
               kills it with a tap,
                    shoves the coveted corpse
                         to the dirt.

          Of course he is out
               and out of his glory,
                    but the runners sing *Hallelujah* louder,
                    feet kissing a new base,
                         arms charismatically raised,
                              honoring their ballpark savior.

The Slide

Takeout

A hit man, you aim
for the infielder's left foot,
upend your second-base enemy,
disrupt the throw, to throw
the double play out of sync.
A macho mob man,
you move menacingly
across the diamond
for the bag.

Figure-4 and Pop-up

Now you're a number,
your straight leg kicking the base
that ticks the scoreboard digits,
flicks the fans' faces to elation.
Or, if still at third and the toss is poor,
use the base as a brace,
and you've moved to another phase,
a "pop-up" pushing you toward home.

Hook

The ball almost gloats, waiting,
but you whoosh in anyway,
your torso rolling away
so it's the lone toe that hooks in
at the finish. Ah, what a slap
on the curve of the ball
when there's only air to tag;
that's all.

Headfirst

Palms down, fingers up,
horizontal and low,
you go for the gusto,
the dirt the sweet sea you dive through.
All you see is speed,
hands grasping the dry, safe base.

LOB

Statistics without the laurel of a score,
you're Left On Base, hopes bashed in
by a last out that left you standing
without a home to dash toward.

You're the suitor abandoned
by the one left holding the bat.
Now those other gents
will swagger in their cool uniforms
past your dusty altar of a plate.

The fans will forget you.
You're gone with the crowd's gruff groans.
Leave quickly. Hide yourself in the outfield.
Forget everything you almost won but didn't.

Double Play

At any angle, a bargain
good enough for Aunt Bessie,
a two-for-one sale that steals
the best of ballet.

Out

is not in,
is not in between,
not in the safety net of safe;
an umpire's yelp;
no horizontal arms halving hot air here;
more than the odd man out;
the orbit of *Oh-Oh-Oh* and *Here-We-Go-Past-the-Park*
all out of the question now;
winning outrun by OW! cut off with a T;
the worst curse from the enemy;
all hard-pitched hope outthrown, thrown out
of luck, of heart, of the hard heat of summer
and what won't be.

Stealing Home

In plain sight of thousands,
ripped right from the catcher's clutch,
home is the ultimate heist,
the grand slam of theft,
the larceny we covet on hot days, cool nights,
when we swear we'd steal the world
for a single tie-breaking run.

Safe

a whole other ballpark,
swoosh of *Yes!* past the ear,
scoreboard clicking wishes against odds
and old men holding out for the opposite.
What-could-be hunkers down here,
dares to snare the numbers,
    spike out the sure thing,
    outlaw the out.
All this dust delivers the done-died-for and dreamed-of:
the sweet whoosh of feet pounding the safety of base.

Grand Slam

Dreams brimming over,
childhood stretched out in legs,
this is the moment replayed on winter days
when frost covers the field,
when age steals away wishes.
Glorious sleep that seeps back there
to the glory of our baseball days.